the T-Shirt book

THE T-SHIRT BOOK

Scott Fresener

Photography by Earl Smith and Nancy Hall

GIBBS·SMITH PUBLISHER

Salt Lake City

First Edition

98   97   96   95   5   4   3   2   1

This is a Peregrine Smith Book, published by
Gibbs Smith, Publisher
P.O. Box 667
Layton, UT 84041

Designed by Randall Smith Associates
Edited by Dawn Valentine Hadlock
Front Cover photo ©1995 Earl Smith & Nancy Hall; shirts courtesy of Grateful Dead Merchandise, Andy's Tees, and Symmetria.
Back Cover photo ©1995 Earl Smith & Nancy Hall; shirts courtesy of Grateful Dead Merchandise, Symmetria, Phoenix Suns and NBA. Elvis and Elvis Presley are registered trademarks of Elvis Presley Enterprises, Inc.

Manufactured in Hong Kong

Library of Congress Cataloging-in-Publication Data
Fresener, Scott.
The T-shirt book / written by Scott Fresener ; photography by Earl
Smith and Nancy Hall.
p. cm.
ISBN 0-87905-686-X
1. T-shirts—History. 2. T-shirts—Collectibles. I. Smith, Earl, 1939- ill. II. Hall, Nancy, 1957- ill. III. Title.
GT2073.S36 1995   95-13401
391—dc20   CIP

DEDICATION

To my wife, Pat.
Scott Fresener

To the memory of Margaret M. Smith, who passed away
during the making of this book. Your light shines on.
Earl Smith and Nancy Hall

ACKNOWLEDGMENTS

I would like to thank my special daughter, Sandy Wong, for her outstanding help as research assistant, scheduler, letter writer, and biggest supporter during this entire project. It wouldn't have come together without her hard work. I would like to thank my wife, Pat, and our kids, Mishelle and Michael, for their help in proofing and research.

I extend my thanks to the many friends and industry colleagues who came through for me with shirts and ideas. I appreciate their time and effort in contributing to the book.

I would also like to thank Russ Cera and Alan Geber at Screened Images; Anna Johnson and Shawn McCready at Superior Embroidery; Denis Meringolo at the Smithsonian Institute; Paul Steward (Waldo); Bob Alabaster and Jeff Gano at Pure Art USA; Melissa Pollack at Carcas Covers; Ken Hunt and Page Simpson at Hanes Printables; Larry Stewart at Stewart's Military Antiques; Steve Mertens at Arizona Images; Headquarters; Fruit of the Loom; Luther Hanson at the U.S. Quartermaster Museum; Walter Bradford at the U.S. Army Center of Military History; Mary Beth at the U.S. Naval Institute; Jim Wilcox from H.O.G. 101; *The New Times*; Fernando Morales at Arizona State University; Cliff Stieglitz at *Airbrush Action* magazine; John Colburn at the Screenprinting and Graphic Imaging Association; Jeff Campos at Electronic Design Group; and Jo Ann Mauck at Art Attacks.

Thanks also go to Dawn Valentine Hadlock at Gibbs Smith, Publisher, for her patience and understanding while working on a short deadline.

CONTENTS

A Rags-to-Riches Story

The T-shirt. What a useful garment. You can wear it to the opera, to work, and to play . . . and when you're done with it, you can use it to wash the car! Who *invented* such a functional piece of clothing anyway?

Although worn mainly by navy men during the first thirty years of the century, the T-shirt became standard issue during World War II. The servicemen brought them home and never gave them up.

What really made the shirt popular was the ability to imprint or decorate it with messages, slogans, and great graphics. Every city and town has a handful of silk screeners who can easily print hundreds or thousands of the same image.

At the same time the youth of the fifties and sixties discovered T-shirts and jeans, they also discovered and created the "walking billboard." For those who weren't very outgoing, the shirt became their voice. For the last forty years, youth have used T-shirts as a vehicle to quickly tell where they go to school, what they think about the current state of politics, their sexual preference, their favorite athlete, their protest against society, and much more. In parts of the country, shirts printed with certain slogans or team names have been banned by schools for fear the shirt showed gang affiliations. A shirt can speak for you. It recycles the thoughts and moods of the day. Even mainstream America buys shirts for themselves or as gifts to show what resorts they've visited, what concerts they've attended, what races they've run.

Once corporate America discovered that a T-shirt was a great promotional product and that people would actually wear a company name on a shirt, the T-shirt became legitimate. Popular restaurants such as the Hard Rock Cafe found they could make almost as much money selling souvenir shirts as food and drink. Shirts are printed for fads, trials (O. J. Simpson), military endeavors (millions of Desert Storm shirts were sold), disasters, products, teams, sporting events ($25 million in Super Bowl shirts!) and, yes, even this book!

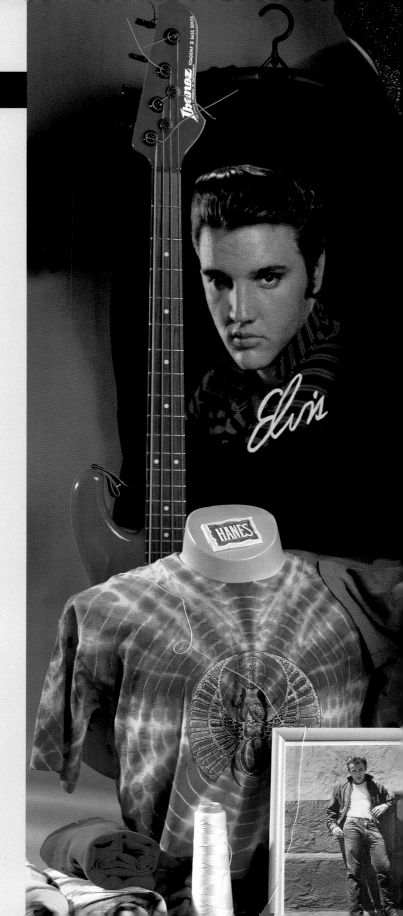

From 500 million shirts sold in 1985, to over one billion sold in 1995, the T-shirt industry has grown up and has its own trade magazines, trade shows, and hundreds of tennis-shoe-and-T-shirt-wearing millionaire entrepreneurs who found gold in T-shirts.

The T-shirt is the marketer's dream: take a $3 T-shirt, put a message on it, sell it for $18—and after it wears out, sell another one. It's functional, disposable, inexpensive, popular, hip, and collectible. You can wear it as a nightshirt, a sport shirt, or an undershirt—with a sports coat, tennis shoes, dress shoes, Levi's, dress pants, or shorts—to work or to play. It's an eight-ounce cotton wonder that brings over $18 billion of revenue per year.

Who invented the T-shirt? We don't know, but whoever you are—thanks! *Hail to the T-shirt!* You've provided a lot of people with a great living and have given the world its most popular garment.

This book has it all. From history, to manufacturing, to decorating . . . with lots of terrific T-shirt photos from Earl Smith and Nancy Hall to tell the story and show the evolution. We have put together the complete *T-Shirt Book* for your amusement, education, and entertainment.

Scott Fresener
Author

Earl Smith and Nancy Hall
Photographers

Every product needs a T-shirt, and this book is no exception. This is the official *T-Shirt Book* T-shirt proudly displayed by the author.

Artwork by Russ Cera/Screened Images.

Elvis and Elvis Presley are registered trademarks of Elvis Presley Enterprises, Inc. © 1995 EPE.

I t's hard to pinpoint exactly when the first T-shirt was produced. It is documented that as early as 1913 the United States Navy adopted the crew-necked, short-sleeved, white cotton undershirt, to be worn under a jumper to cover sailors' chest hairs.

At that point, the T-shirt was definitely an undergarment. Even then, however, the T-shirt was not the undergarment for the average workingman. He was still wearing a sleeveless undershirt called a "singlet," or a single-piece "union suit" almost into the forties. It wasn't until the late thirties that companies such as Hanes, Sears Roebuck, and Fruit of the Loom earnestly started to market the T-shirt. (Fruit of the Loom didn't actually start to knit shirts until 1938.)

It is reported that the T-shirt (and union suit) received a major setback in 1934, when Clark Gable took off his dress shirt to reveal a bare torso in the movie *It Happened One Night*. Although his costar, Claudette Colbert, was not impressed, American women liked the bare-chest look—and men followed Gable's lead.

A 1937 Consumer's Union Report lists "cotton under-shirts" and "cotton union suits" as separate categories and shows undershirts with names like "Skivvies" and "jimshirts." They were only 1.5 to 2 ounces back then—a far cry from today's heavy-weight T-shirt that can weigh as much as 8 ounces. By 1940, the Consumer's Union Report had dropped the "cotton union suit" category.

In 1938, Sears introduced a T-shirt for only 24 cents apiece. It was called a "gob" shirt (a gob is a sailor) and was proclaimed to be either an outer garment or an undershirt— "It's practical, correct either way."

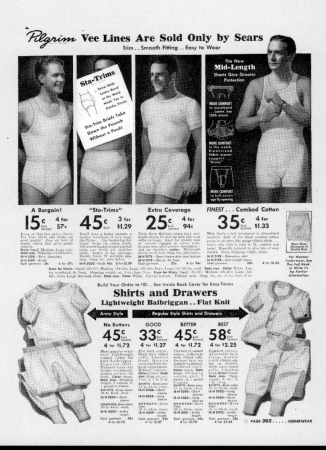

▲ **A SEARS CATALOG** from 1941 shows army-style T-shirts for only 45 cents and regular T-shirts for 25 cents.

◄ **HANES SHIRTS AND DRAWERS AD 1902**

This is where it all started. From this full-body union suit of 1902—to short briefs with elastic (Lastex) to hold them up and a short-sleeved T-shirt in the thirties. They actually wore these things back then?

Photo courtesy of Hanes, Winston-Salem, NC.

THE NAVY first introduced what came to be ►
called the navy T-style shirt around 1913.

Photo courtesy of U.S. Naval Institute, Annapolis, MD.

While it is widely recounted that the army had T-shirts early in the war, it was really the marines who first issued the navy T-type shirt. It didn't take the marines long to realize that white was an easy target, however, so the early white navy T-type shirts were dyed in the field with coffee grounds! Later the men were issued sage-green shirts.

The army didn't actually get their own navy T-type shirts until late in the war and after. A 1944 study from the Quartermaster of Clothing and Equipment for the Tropics shows that the army was still field-testing T-shirts and sleeve-less undershirts to see which the men preferred. In the field test, the men preferred the navy T-type shirt because it had a better appearance, was more comfortable due to greater absorption under the arms, was more comfortable when worn with backpacks, and provided greater protection from sunburn.

When the servicemen returned from war, the shirts came home with them—and the Skivvies, jimshirt, and gob shirt were here to stay.

During World War II, the T-shirt was more for function than fashion. The early-issue military shirts had a much wider neck and shorter sleeve than today's full-cut shirt, and they were a much tighter fit than today's full cut. This tight-fitting style remained much the same from the early 1900s through the sixties.

The late forties saw the first printed T-shirts. The Smithsonian Institute's oldest printed shirt reads "Dew-It with Dewey"—from New York Governor Thomas E. Dewey's 1948 presidential campaign.

The T-shirt got a real boost from underwear to outerwear when Marlon Brando showed his form in a tight-fitting T-shirt in the 1951 movie *A Streetcar Named Desire*. Thanks, Stanley Kowalski, for giving the T-shirt sex appeal!

Brando again set the stage with his T-shirt-and-jeans rebel in the 1954 movie *The Wild One*, and his cultural partner James Dean continued the look in 1955 with the classic movie *Rebel without a Cause*. OK, Elvis just happened along then also and showed the world how hip a T-shirt and leather jacket could be.

About that time, the T-shirt style also changed a little—the neck opening became smaller. The fit was still tight, though, and the sleeves were still short enough to show off a man's physique. T-shirts were still a very male piece of clothing.

That's when clever marketers such as Walt Disney and Roy Rogers saw the possibilities of the printed T-shirt as a souvenir. Just think—it's a useful piece of clothing, it's inexpensive, and it has a short life span. Perfect!

In the early 1950s, such innovators as Ed Roth (aka "Big Daddy Roth") and Carl Smith (aka "Big Daddy Rat") started to screen print and airbrush shirts with car designs. Back then, the "ink" used was house paint and spray paint.

In the fifties, most college shirts and sport shirts were decorated with cloth letters or with "flocking," a process through which thin fibers of rayon were electrostatically embedded in an adhesive printed on the shirt. This was a very slow and messy process that was just waiting to be replaced.

In 1959, a new ink called "plastisol" was invented. This ink was more durable and stretchable—and brought about the birth of T-shirt printing as we know it today.

The sixties provided the background for statement shirts, tie-dyed shirts, and freedom of speech. The British rock 'n' roll invasion and Vietnam were the perfect partners for a newfound culture, and the printed T-shirt was the perfect vehicle of

choice for expression. The peace symbol was the most popular T-shirt image. It was easier to wear a statement on your chest than to carry a picket sign. As free love, long hair, and drugs prevailed, tie-dyed shirts that could be custom designed in your kitchen sink—with no investment—were the thing. The Woodstock generation loved T-shirts!

In the late sixties, T-shirts were sold mainly at state fairs, car shows, and special events—but the lowly T-shirt that had been a fad in the sixties suddenly grew up in the seventies. The iron-on transfer made it easy to pick a design, pick a shirt, and combine the two using a household iron.

The T-shirt store, as we know it, didn't exist until the early seventies. The iron-on transfer made it easy to mass-produce thousands of different designs, and every mall and shopping center had its T-shirt store. Early T-shirt stores were not much more sophisticated than state fair displays, however, and it wasn't uncommon for upscale malls to tell merchants they didn't want any T-shirt stores.

In the late seventies, a new photo-realistic iron-on transfer called a "litho transfer" was developed. It revolutionized the quality of the graphic images that could now be printed on shirts. One of the earliest and most popular litho transfers was of Farrah Fawcett of TV's *Charlie's Angels* fame. This was the most popular T-shirt of 1977, selling more than $8 million worth!

It all came together when entrepreneur Bill Windsor started a magazine called *Impressions* in 1978 and followed it in 1979 with a T-shirt trade show called The Imprinted Sportswear Shows. At the same time, my wife, Pat, and I wrote what became the bible of the industry, *How to Print T-Shirts for Fun and Profit*. Suddenly, T-shirts had become an industry!

The eighties started the great graphics craze. Artists who had shunned the T-shirt now found a new canvas! Prices of $2,000 and higher for a design became a reality, because great graphics sold shirts. Corporations also found a new vehicle for their message, and the era of shirts giving free advertising started. Imagine, people will actually wear your company's name on their chest like a walking billboard and pay for the privilege! Great concept! Rock 'n' roll and sporting event promoters discovered that the bottom line could be much much larger with merchandise sales, and the licensing business flourished into the billion-dollar business it is today.

MARLON BRANDO
showed that a working-class stiff, Stanley Kowalski, could be a sex symbol in his tight-fitting T-shirt in the 1951 classic *A Streetcar Named Desire*. He again glorified the rebellious youth theme with his jacket, T-shirt, and jeans in 1954 in *The Wild One*.

▶ **THE NAVY INTRODUCED THEM,** the marines got them first, and finally the army had its T-shirt too.

IN 1948, THE P. H. HANES ▼ Knitting Mills was in full swing making T-shirts that sold for $1.00. P. H. Hanes would be surprised that the company is now owned by Sara Lee. Maybe the theme of the nineties should be "a cake with every shirt."

Photo courtesy of Hanes, Winston-Salem, NC.

◀ **JAMES DEAN** showed the T-shirt for what it was: a rebellion against tradition and against everything adults were for. In the 1955 movie *Rebel without a Cause*, he glorified the T-shirt-and-jeans look of the fifties.

The eighties also liked free expression on a shirt. Hand-decorated shirts, tie-dyed shirts, and even a process called "spin art" were in. Shirt sizes got bigger as everyone wanted a looser, baggier look. The consumer also wanted larger and softer designs. The rubbery and not very wash-resistant iron-on transfer practically died in the early eighties. As colored T-shirts became more popular, stores started carrying preprinted shirts, known in the industry as "preprints" or "stock designs." Newer printing methods let shirt designs puff, glitter, glow, and change color—and consumers kept coming back for more.

The nineties continued with better graphics and with major corporations buying into the business. Sara Lee bought Hanes, Champion Products, and Stedman. In 1993 Fruit of the Loom paid close to $150 million for Salem Sportswear, a company that two friends had started in 1980 with a $450 investment!

The early nineties also saw the resurgence of the iron-on transfer—now called a "heat transfer." They were softer, puffier, and more durable—and they could duplicate the quality of a direct screen print.

Today's T-shirt business is a conglomeration of T-shirt mills, screen printers, embroiderers, and airbrushers. The computer has made it possible to do outstanding photo-realistic designs in quantities as small as one shirt. New printing processes using ink-jet technology are in the developmental stages by companies such as Xerox. These new systems may revolutionize how a shirt is decorated.

The Internet has spawned a whole new line of concept shirts, called "Cybershirts," with your own personal E-mail address or "cyberspeak" emblazoned on them. The Internet has also become the T-shirt mall of the future, and you can now order any shirt imaginable, including custom printing—online!

The T-shirt. An $18 billion industry. From undershirt to everyday piece of clothing. From plain to terrific graphics. From cute to raunchy. Buying T-shirts is like taking pictures: they tell the world where you have been and who you are. If only they lasted longer, they would be an anthropologist's dream.

▼ **THE WOODSTOCK** generation started with more than 500,000 attendees at Woodstock in 1969. If it worked once, then why not again in 1994? A souvenir shirt from the original Woodstock is almost impossible to find.

Shirt and poster courtesy of Woodstock Ventures, Inc./Polygram Diversified Ventures, Inc., under license to Great Entertainment Merchandise Inc.

◀ **IN THE SIXTIES,** tie-dyed shirts said it all. Now our kids are wearing tie-dyes as if they were a brand-new phenomenon, and some of us old hippies are wondering what happened to the last thirty years. Some things never go out of style. The current rage is to combine beautiful tie-dyes from the sixties with nineties screen-print graphics.

Shirts courtesy of Eye-Dye, Pensacola, FL. Model: Cinnamon Wells.

THIS WAS THE DESIGN ▶

that the industry credits with making the T-shirt legitimate. It could have also been that Farrah Fawcett was the poster girl of the seventies, and millions of Farrah admirers bought over $8 million worth of her pinup

Shirt courtesy of Pro Arts Inc. ©1976.

15

◄**EVEN A WAR** needs shirts, and Desert Storm made a lot of T-shirt sellers rich. Unfortunately, when the war ended, hundreds of thousands of Desert Storm shirts had to be dumped at flea markets.

Shirt courtesy of the Waldo collection.

WHO WOULD HAVE ►

thought a bunch of hippie musicians in the sixties would still be playing in their fifties? From corporate America to free spirits, Dead Heads have purchased millions of Grateful Dead shirts.

Shirt courtesy of Grateful Dead Merchandise.

needs a shirt, and $25 million of these shirts is a pretty good reason to print them. From 25 cents in the thirties to $19.95 in the nineties.

Shirt by Starter. Trademark and © NFL.

THE SCREEN-PRINTING ▶

process changed from simple paper stencils to a high-tech photographic process that can produce all the colors of the rainbow. This outstanding shirt is from award-winning printer Andy Anderson of Anderson Studios in Nashville.

CHAPTER 2

From Raw Cotton to Finished Garments

The T-shirt. You buy it, wear it, wash it, and then use it as a rag. But how is it actually made? T-shirt manufacturing is a fairly complex process that can take months to get from raw cotton to a finished garment. In between, you have yarn making, knitting, dyeing, cutting, sewing, and many other processes that turn a plant into a wearable garment.

Garments are made of twisted strands of yarn that are knitted into fabric. This yarn can be natural material (such as vegetable-fiber cotton), manmade material (such as the polymer known as polyester), or a combination of both—called a blend.

Cotton

Cotton is a soft, cool material that absorbs moisture and is comfortable to wear. Cotton fibers are long, porous, and somewhat hollow, with concentric layers or walls that readily absorb perspiration and draw it away from the body in a process called "wicking."

Cotton fibers are noted for their warmth in cold weather, too. The fibers protect against the wind without trapping body moisture. They tend to insulate because of the cushion of air that helps give them a soft feel. Synthetic fabrics, on the other hand, have smooth, slick surfaces that touch the skin and do not insulate well.

In the last few years, the major mills have done an excellent job of producing quality 100 percent cotton shirts. Shrinkage is controlled by chemically treating the cotton with resins and stabilizers—or through special processing techniques called "compacting." The consumer now has a much better opinion of cotton than ever before.

Cotton yarn is made by spinning or twisting the fibrous hairs of cotton into lengths of yarn. Before it is spun, the cotton is cleansed of foreign matter, short fibers, seeds, and tangles by a method called "carding."

After the carding process, the cotton is drawn and, if necessary, blended with synthetic fibers. From this process, it may be combed before it is spun into yarn. The combing

▼ **COTTON** is one of the most important textile fibers in the world. An average T-shirt contains up to ½ pound of cotton fibers.

▼ **ECO FIBRE** (TM) T-shirts made from 100 percent recycled cotton, wool, and other waste fibers help save over five billion pounds of textile waste from landfills each year.

Shirt courtesy of Equipoise, Burnsville, MN.

process removes fibers that are too short and immature along with any remaining foreign particles.

After being combed, the cotton is reduced in size to a thick cordlike material in a process called "roving." It is then spun and twisted into the proper yarn size. The more yarn is twisted, the stiffer it becomes. This spinning or twisting process draws the fibers down to the predetermined size, called the yarn number.

100 Percent Recycled Cotton

The shirt-making process has never been very environmentally friendly, and many manufacturers are now jumping on the eco-conscious bandwagon. A patented Eco Fibre (TM) process recycles the cotton material that is wasted between the cotton fields and the sewed products. These billions of pounds of waste that would normally overflow our landfills are turned into special environmentally friendly "green" T-shirts.

Organically Grown Cotton

Another environmentally conscious shirt is made of 100 percent pure organic cotton that is grown without synthetic pesticides, herbicides, or chemical fertilizers. In the manufacturing process, beeswax is used to spin the yarn, and environmentally friendly chemicals are used to finish the fabric.

Pop Bottle Shirts

Yes, you read it right. There is now a special yarn—made from recycled plastic pop bottles—that is being knitted into a fairly soft and comfortable T-shirt. These shirts are made from 50 percent polyethylene terephthalate (also known as PET) and 50 percent virgin polyester.

Polyester

Polyester was commercially introduced in 1953 by DuPont. Simply put, it is a man-made fiber derived from coal, air, water, and petroleum. Polyester is made into yarn by cutting the thin extruded filaments of thread into short staple lengths—and then twisting and spinning these filaments into yarn. Polyester fibers are very durable, but because they are a slicker, nonporous fiber, they do not absorb moisture or insulate as well as cotton.

▶ **100 PERCENT PURE ORGANICALLY GROWN** cotton shirts are environmentally friendly. No pesticides, herbicides, or chemical fertilizers are used during growing.

Shirts courtesy of Planet Vision, Las Vegas, NV.

▲ **DRINK YOUR COKE** and wear it too! The latest environmental craze is to make shirts from recycled plastic pop bottles that are chopped up, heated, and turned into pellets. The pellets are then extruded in fibers used for yarn.

Shirts courtesy of ECO Options, Charlotte, NC, and Signs & Symbols, Brunswick, ME.

Cotton/Polyester Blends

A 50/50 blend shirt is popular because it combines the good qualities of both cotton and polyester. Cotton/polyester blends offer the comfort and moisture absorption of cotton and the durability and shrinkage resistance of polyester. The blending of the yarn is generally done before the combing and spinning process. This creates what is called an "intimate" blend.

Knitting

Fabric weaving is done by interlacing yarn at right angles—the process used for yard goods, sheets, and most cloth. Knitting is done by interlooping yarn, using needles (similar to hand-knitting a sweater). T-shirt material is always knit- ted in what is called a

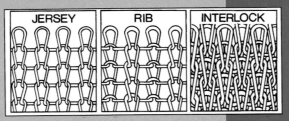

JERSEY   RIB   INTERLOCK

circular knit or a round tube form. This eliminates the need for the garment to have seams down the sides. Three differ- ent stitches are generally used in knitting T-shirt material: jersey, rib, and interlock knit.

"Jersey knit" (also called "plain knit") is used for basic T-shirts. It produces a smooth material with a fine pattern of vertical lines on the outside ("wales") and horizontal rows ("courses") on the inside.

"Rib knit" produces wales on both sides of the cloth, because every other course loop drops to the back of the knit. This 1x1 rib knit gives the garment much more elasticity than a jersey knit.

"Interlock knit" is a special run-resistant knit that com- bines two inter-knitted 1x1 rib fabrics. It is less elastic than rib or jersey knit and has a smooth surface on both sides. It is used for ladies' tops, some children's garments, and better- quality shirts. Because of the increased yarn content and the more complicated knit, interlock material is more expensive.

▼ **MOST T-SHIRTS** are made with a standard jersey knit. Rib knits have more elastic- ity; interlock knits are heavier.

PLASTIC pop bottle shirts are part of ▼ the solution, not the problem.

Shirt courtesy of ECO Options, Charlotte, NC.

ECO OPTIONS

...A UNIQUE CONCEPT IN CLOTHING COMPOSED OF RECYCLED PLASTIC BOTTLES. P. E. T. PRODUCTS FROM ECO OPTIONS ARE BREATHABLE, WICKABLE AND HIGHLY DURABLE. WASTE THAT WOULD NORMALLY BECOME PART OF THE LANDFILL IS TRANSFORMED INTO WEARABLE FABRICS. THIS SHIRT IS PART OF THE SOLUTION NOT THE POLLUTION!

REDUCE ✿ RECYCLE ✿ REUSE ✿ REGENERATE

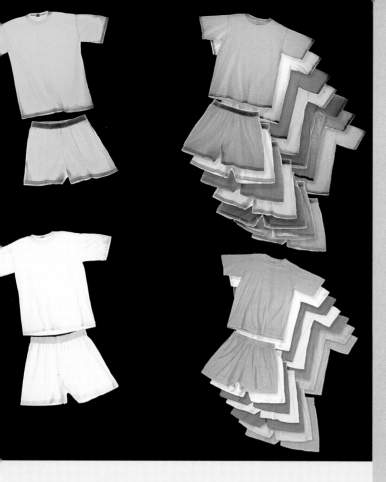

Fabric Finish

After the fabric is knitted, it is referred to as "greige goods." This fabric is inspected on large light tables. After inspection, all greige goods are bleached or scoured to help eliminate color variations in the cotton and to allow the yarn to shrink.

Dyeing

Fabric dyeing is an art in itself that can be very time consuming. Since the dyes used in cotton are different than those used in polyester blends, the two are dyed in different formulations. One stage dyes the cotton portion, and the other dyes the polyester. Knit material is generally dyed in large vats that work under heat and pressure. Dark colors have to stay in the vats longer than lighter colors. As a comparison, light colors may stay in the dye solution for five hours, while dark colors may stay in for sixteen hours or more.

Shrinkage Control

After drying, the fabric is calendered—a process that uses steam to bring the fabric to the desired width. This process, sometimes called "preshrinking," helps control fabric shrinkage. With current calendering and compacting processes, fabric shrinkage on 100 percent cotton garments can be held to less than 3 percent.

Cutting

Finished tubular knitted goods are laid out on long cutting tables in stacks that are as many as 400 to 500 plies thick. The desired pattern is hand-marked on the top ply, and specific pieces are cut out using special electric knives that have extremely sharp blades and that operate somewhat like a saber saw. Some of the larger manufacturers now use state-of-the-art "cookie cutter" presses to die-cut the fabric in a much more automated process.

Garment Assembly

Sewing garments is very labor intensive. It is not nearly as automated as you might think. In fact, the actual sewing operations consist of rooms of workers sewing shirts together with industrial sewing machines, much like the sewing was done around the turn of the century.

All of this work for a garment that wholesales for around $3.00!

▲ **YES, THEY EVEN MAKE** glow-in-the-dark shirts that are great for night joggers, bicyclists, and the nightclub scene.
Photo courtesy of Color Magic, Orlando, FL.

▼ **SHIRT MATERIAL** is cut in stacks that are 400 to 500 plies thick, using knives that operate like saber saws. Modern factories use "cookie cutter" die-cutting to cut the shirt pieces.

CHAPTER 3

Decorating Methods

Face it. Would you pay $20 for a blank T-shirt? No! You pay $20 because of the graphic or image on the shirt. This image could be anything from a simple hand-painted design, to an embroidered logo, a tie-dye of the entire shirt, or a detailed screen-printed graphic. It is the graphic, image, or embellishment that sells T-shirts.

T-shirt Artists

Decorating a garment has evolved from simple dyeing and hand-painting methods to intricate lifelike printing. In the sixties and seventies, being a T-shirt artist was associated with being a free spirit or a rebel without a cause. It wasn't a glamorous job and certainly didn't pay well. Today's artists view the T-shirt as a canvas, and creating great designs is a legitimate business. In the seventies, an industry veteran known as Spider received $50 for a complete design. Now that same piece of art goes for $500 to $1000.

Creating T-shirt art has evolved from the tedious process of hand drawing a design to the much more productive and accurate computer graphics. Nowadays, the first question an employer asks an artist is "Do you know computer graphics?"

Screen Printing

One of the oldest-known printing processes—invented in China over 4,000 years ago—screen printing is actually very simple. When done correctly, it produces a bright, detailed graphic. Although the screen-printing process is used for a wide variety of materials from wood, to plastic and metal, T-shirts account for over 60 percent of all the screen printing being done.

Screen printing is done by stretching a piece of polyester fabric onto a wood or metal frame. Although the process is generally called silk screening, silk is rarely used in the modern screen-printing shop.

A stencil of the design is photographically created on the fabric. Then special water-based or rubberized textile inks are pushed through the stencil with a rubber blade, called a "squeegee." The basics of the process haven't really changed in hundreds of years.

There are approximately 30,000 active screen printers in the U.S., many of them garage operations servicing local schools, businesses, and clubs.

Larger screen-printing companies use automatic presses that can print up to 70 dozen shirts per hour! In fact, companies such as Winterland, who specialize in licensed rock 'n' roll shirts, can print over 150,000 shirts per day! Due to the high production possible with the automatic presses, screen printing is the most popular decorating method for mass-produced garments. The ability to imprint a garment cheaply has been responsible for the explosive growth of the T-shirt industry.

Heat Transfers

This is basically a screen-printing process, but the printing is done on special release paper, and the image is applied to a garment with a heat-transfer press. Heat transfers are very popular because a T-shirt store can keep a minimal inventory and just apply a graphic to a blank shirt when the customer picks out a design.

▼ SCREEN PRINTING IS DONE BY PUSHING INK THROUGH A STENCIL THAT IS HELD IN PLACE WITH POLYESTER FABRIC ON A CARRIER FRAME.

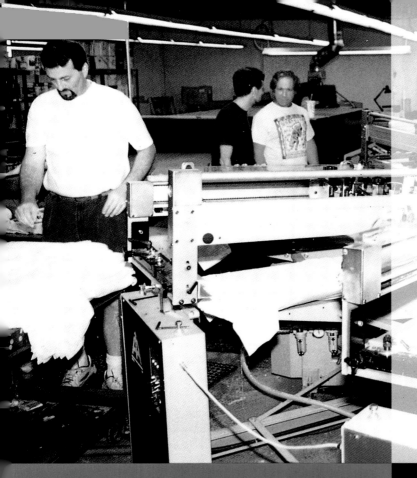

◄ **PURE ART USA** in Scottsdale, AZ, specializes in reproducing fine-art prints and beautiful photo-realistic images on garments. They can screen print thousands of shirts per day on automatic equipment.

Run by Jeff Gano (left) and Bob Alabaster (right), Pure Art is an award-winning company doing work for companies such as Guess and The Gap.

Embroidery

Like screen printing, embroidery on shirts has evolved from a hand operation with limited production to an entire industry. Some embroidery machines cost well over $100,000 and are capable of producing thousands of the same design. Since the mid-eighties, embroidery has seen tremendous growth.

Computerization changed the process from a simple single-head machine that could stitch names on bowling shirts, to machines with twenty-five identical heads using up to ten needles per head—and capable of making thousands of stitches per minute, per head.

▲ **THE T-SHIRT BOOK** T-shirt being printed on an automatic printing press.

▶ **EMBROIDERED DESIGNS** have a rich, quality look and feel that make them perfect for corporate logos. Designs like these have thousands of stitches for each color and can take up to thirty minutes to sew on automatic embroidery machines.

Shirts courtesy of Superior Embroidery, Phoenix, AZ.

TIE-DYE PAUL, WHOSE REAL NAME IS PAUL LITTLE, travels around the country to Renaissance festivals and fairs selling intricately decorated garments that he has spent days and weeks creating.

Although they appear to be tie-dyed, Paul's designs use a combination of traditional tying with thousand-year-old Oriental stitching and banding techniques—called "shibori" and "tratik." He may spend days tying and stitching a single garment in preparation for the dyes.

He then applies the dyes using squeeze bottles, paint brushes, syringes, and traditional vat dying. His workshop is the great outdoors at whatever fair or festival he happens to be attending.

Using these methods, Paul is able to create intricate lacelike images and patterns that make each garment truly special to own and wear.

Tie-dye

Tie-dyed shirts became the rage in the sixties because no two shirts were alike, and anyone could dye a shirt in the kitchen sink. The process involves twisting and tying the shirt with rubber bands or thread, and then dyeing it. Tie-dyeing has evolved into an art form, with detailed intricate designs that can take days to create—just for one shirt! Although the height of tie-dye's popularity was the sixties, the late eighties saw a resurgence of tie-dye among the kids of the free-love generation.

Wearable Art

The term "wearable art" was coined in the mid-eighties, when hand-done shirts were popular because of their individuality. Thousands of people started home-based, part-time T-shirt businesses—applying glitter, foil, rhinestones, pieces of cloth, and other embellishments to garments and selling them to friends and specialty department stores. With minimal investment and a little imagination, anyone could start a business. Consumers still want and love a one-of-a-kind hand-decorated garment. Although the process is still popular, the profitability has largely disappeared for the at-home artist because large manufacturers can produce hand-done shirts in large quantities.

▲ **THE TERM** "wearable art" was coined for shirts that were painstakingly hand-decorated with foil, glitter, cloth, rhinestones, and other embellishments.

Airbrushing on T-shirts

Airbrushed shirts have been around since the early fifties, when the process became an art form at car shows. The street-rod airbrushers and pin-stripers discovered that they could use the same process to paint directly on clothing. In the seventies, every state fair had a T-shirt booth and an airbrush person painting names on shirts.

Airbrushing is also a fairly simple process. Using a special paint sprayer—called an airbrush—and a compressor, the artist actually spray paints the image onto the shirt. The airbrush allows the artist great control over the amount of paint and the detail possible, and with a quick change of the paint bottle, another color can be sprayed. Airbrushing is still a very popular art form and can be used to create very lifelike images on T-shirts. Original hand-airbrushed shirts sell for $50 to $100—or even much higher from well-known artists.

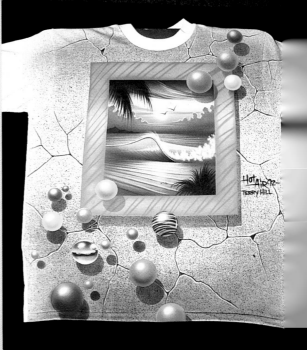

AIRBRUSH ARTIS EXTRAORDINAIRE TERRY HILL is one of the air

brush industry's most outstanding and popular artists. He has been painting shirts since 1981 an is a feature instructor at *Airbrush Action* Magazine's Airbrush Getaways around the count Terry airbrushes T-shirts in his store, appropriately named Hot Air, in the T-shirt airbrush capit of the world—Fort Walton Beach, FL. He also works occasional fairs and car shows and makes airbrushing on T-shirts look like fun!

Shirts © Terry Hill.
Photos courtesy of *Airbrush Action* magazine.

▲ **AN AIR-BRUSH** is no more than a precision paint sprayer with a lever on top to control the amount of paint spraying out.

◀ **OTHER** methods of decorating include dip-dyeing, marbleizing, block printing—and wax batik, such as this shirt.

Shirt courtesy of Batik Jim.
Model: Michael Fresener.

CHAPTER 4

The Imprinted Sportswear Industry

Although the name Imprinted Sportswear Industry implies that all garments are printed, the name has become synonymous with any method of decorating a T-shirt. What was once a loose band of entrepreneurs doing their own thing has evolved into an $18-billion industry.

The lowly T-shirt, which legitimate business people once looked down upon, has gained respect. When companies like Sara Lee bought Hanes, and MCA bought Winterland, the industry knew that their time had come.

The official trade association for screen printers is the Screenprinting and Graphic Imaging Association (formerly the Screen Printing Association). SGIA has thousands of members worldwide. Although many members print more than just T-shirts, over half of the membership is comprised of T-shirt printers. SGIA has a yearly trade show and convention that has become the meeting ground for the industry. At this show, awards of excellence are given to the best printers, and it is an honor to receive a Golden Imaging Award for outstanding work.

The industry also believes in giving something back. The official charity of the Imprinted Sportswear Industry is Variety Clubs International. Through charity auctions and industry contributions, over $1 million has been raised to benefit needy children. Most of the money has been used to provide "Sunshine Coaches" for clubs and organizations that transport children to and from doctor's visits, school programs, therapy, and other necessary destinations.

Success breeds copycats, and the T-shirt business has its share of bootlegging and even counterfeiting of legitimate designs. The problem has become so rampant—especially in the licensed sports and rock 'n' roll areas—that an anti-bootlegging coalition was formed, called CAPS (Coalition to Advance the Protection of Sports Logos). Its members consist of the NFL, NBA, NHL, MLB, and other concerned companies and associations. Millions of dollars of illegal merchandise is seized yearly, both within the U.S. and by the U.S. Customs.

▼ **MAJOR MILLS** such as Hanes have large displays of their latest products at industry trade shows.

◀ **SINCE 1978,** there has been a prolif-
eration of specialized trade magazines, with such
names as *Impressions, ScreenPlay, Imprintables
Today, Imprinting Business, Embroidery Business
News, The Press, Airbrush Action Magazine,* and
more.

▼ **THE POPULARITY** of decorated
shirts has also created a vast network of T-shirt
wholesalers who sell blank shirts to local screen
printers and embroiderers. Jewel & Co. in Landover,
MD, brags of having an extremely heavyweight tee.
Actually the "tee" is a five-foot-tall, 680-pound
bronze statue of a T-shirt that sits in front of their
70,000 blank T-shirt warehouse.

**THE U.S. SCREEN
PRINTING INSTITUTE**
was founded by my wife and I in 1979. We have
taught more than 8,000 people the art and craft
of screen printing. Our book *How to Print T-
Shirts for Fun and Profit* has sold more than
100,000 copies. Many of the screen-printing
industry's largest printers started out at the
institute.

CHAPTER 5

T-Shirts and Fashion

So what exactly is fashion? One definition is "the current style or custom, as in dress or behavior."

The T-shirt fits right in. You can wear it as casual attire and be in fashion if it is the current style for your group or peers. Or you can wear it when dressing up. Frankly, you could wear a T-shirt almost anywhere today and be socially correct, as long as it is clean and the image is not objectionable.

Even fashion designers have discovered that by putting their label on a blank shirt and selling it at upscale, trendy department stores, they can get $30 or more. Put a simple graphic on the shirt, and the price goes up.

Although Marlon, James, and Elvis got the craze going, it took a lot longer for the T-shirt to become an accepted fashion item—one not scorned by adults and conservatives as an objectionable statement of rebellion.

Remember how Clark Gable's bare chest in 1934 had an effect on fashion? Things don't change. People wear what they see. Fashion . . . the current style or custom.

If wearing a tie-dye or outrageous slogan was the "current style" of the sixties and seventies, then it could be said that these were the fashions of those two decades.

It really wasn't until the late seventies that the disco craze prompted people to mix and match clothes and wear fancy but nontraditional attire. The 1977 hit *Saturday Night Fever*, with John Travolta, was at the peak of the "let's dance" craze. Remember the Village People and their outrageous outfits and tight-fitting T-shirts?

That same year, *Annie Hall*, an Oscar-winning Woody Allen film, started the new layered look when Diane Keaton dressed with loose-fitting layers of clothes.

This loose look became more popular and started a craze that would last for years when Jennifer Beals draped a cut-up sweatshirt over her shoulder in the 1983 movie *Flashdance*. Designers got their scissors out and started to cut, rip, and tear shirts. Sales of torn shirts, tights, and leg warmers went through the roof.

By the late eighties, women were designing their own shirts, using foil, rhinestones, glitter, pieces of cloth, and

▲ THE FASHION GARMENT

of the West Coast is, and has been, a pair of baggies or shorts and a heavyweight T-shirt with a surfing scene.

Model: Eric Ruelas.

anything else they could glue onto a shirt. An entire industry of very fashionable one-of-a-kind shirts, produced on people's dining room tables, was born—called "wearable art."

The T-shirt has even taken on fine art. Prints from the masters, such as van Gogh, Picasso, and Michelangelo, are being reproduced on T-shirts and sold in very modern, upscale T-shirt stores.

It has been hard for manufacturers to keep up with the current trends. In the mid-eighties, sizes changed from an even range of small through extra-large shirts to a larger, looser cut. Could it be that the baby boomers were getting a little heavier? It took the mills years to adjust to the newer size scale. Today the most popular sizes are large, extra-large, and even bigger. Shirts are looser, and imprinted graphics cover the entire front of the shirt.

Colors change, too. Predominately white T-shirts were replaced by colored shirts years ago, yet white is still the most popular color. The color of the nineties is black. With great graphics and improved printing techniques, a design will jump off a black shirt. Other colors are more trendy. One year, fluorescents are in. The next, earth tones more popular. Each year the mills introduce new colors—and cross their fingers.

Today's styles are a little reminiscent of the layered, baggy look of *Annie Hall* fame. This new "grunge" look—found mainly on teens and preteens—consists of oversized T-shirts with long, baggy shorts, a long-sleeve shirt around the waist, and a baseball cap worn backwards. If long pants are worn, it is desirable to have the legs ventilated with holes in the knees.

On the female side, the trend is back to tight-fitting ladies' T-shirts with short skirts. (Sounds like the seventies to me!)

Another grungier, rock 'n' roll look for both males and females is to shave your head and wear tattoos and lots of jewelry in various pierced parts of your body. One earring per ear is just not cool. The T-shirt needs to be of your favorite group, and it doesn't have to be neat and ironed. Wrinkled, torn, and with holes is all the better.

What will it be tomorrow? If the current trend toward seventies' styles and designs continues, then shirt sizes and graphics will get smaller. A recent visit to T-shirt stores in selected cities showed a surprising increase in seventies graphics, such as Farrah Fawcett, the Brady Bunch, the Jackson Five, Charlie's Angels, the Monkees, and other designs we thought were long dead. Even the older, rubbery litho transfers that had glitter around the images were on the racks. (In the old days, we called these "litho-glitter combo transfers.") Remember designs like "Class of '75," " '79 TransAm," and other classics? The shirts were also reminiscent of this era, with the hot seller being a ringer shirt—a white shirt with a colored collar and sleeve band.

There is also a lot of tie-dye again. As long as Jerry Garcia and his band of Dead are touring, this fashion item will be a staple of the industry.

Respected schools—such as the Fashion Institute of Technology in New York—have presented traveling exhibits on the T-shirt in fashion. The National Museum of American History has a T-shirt collection in its section on Costume, Community Life, and Political History.

Unless cotton becomes outlawed, T-shirts will always be in fashion.

◀▲ **YES, YOU TOO** can make your own shirts. Glue on some rhinestones, sew on a little fabric or some flowers, sprinkle on some glitter, and you have a one-of-a-kind fashion item of wearable art. Now if they could only mass produce these things!

ALL IT TOOK to make your own
Flashdance shirt in 1983 was a T-shirt or sweatshirt
and a pair of scissors. Cut out the neck, trim the sleeves, cut the
seam, get real crazy—and you had the fashion statement of the day.

Background Photo: Model Nancy Hall, Signature Model and Talent Agency,
Phoenix, AZ.

31

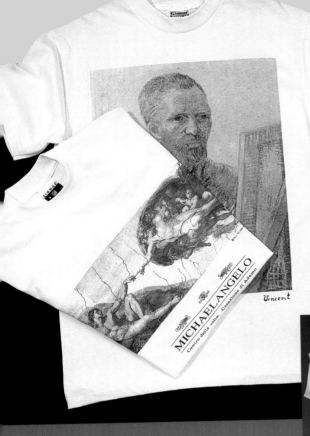

◀ YOU CALL THIS ART?

If the T-shirt is a canvas, then this is art. Pure Art of Scottsdale, AZ, specializes in offering art on T-shirts. They print museum-quality prints of the masters on the most popular canvas around.

Even their stores are not just your average T-shirt store. The shirts are not hung on racks—they are individually framed, and they have picture-frame lights on them. What a concept! Call it art and charge more money for it. It must be fashion.

Shirts courtesy of Pure Art, USA.

▶ THESE PUNK KIDS reflect

how fashion trends affect even our kids.

Shirt courtesy of Pure Art, USA.

IF PIERCED EARS, nose, or ▶

other body parts is your thing, and you like the feel of stubble on your head, then this is the fashion statement to make.

Your parents won't like it—but then they aren't the ones you are trying to impress anyway.

Model: Jill Haarlander.

▲ **BAGGY SHORTS** and loose-fitting T-shirt—the fashion look of the nineties. Throw in a seventies image on the shirt, and you'll fit right in.

Air guitar model Bret Mattingly courtesy of Signature Model and Talent, Phoenix, AZ.

CHAPTER 6

T-Shirts with a Message

We could fill a book ten times this size with message T-shirts from every walk of life and from every political and religious persuasion and ideology. Message shirts are a little different than slogan shirts. A slogan can be a message—but is generally something cute or obscene or a play on words. A message T-shirt, on the other hand, should get you to think. The message needs to have meaning or arouse the soul. The shirt shows that the wearer is passionate enough about the message to tell the world his or her true feelings.

Rather than displaying a sampling of message shirts from over the years, we have chosen to include message shirts that speak for our current times—messages on the state of our society today, as we and the shirt designers see it.

▼ WITH LAWYER BASHING

a current rage, there is no better way to vent your frustration with them than on a shirt.

Shirt courtesy of High Cotton Inc.

34

THE GRAPEVINE

HELPS THE HOMELESS HELP THEMSELVES

B. 8TH - 14TH

50¢

THESE SHIRTS were printed by Ashbury Images of San Francisco, CA, a nonprofit organization dedicated to helping those who have been homeless and who are building their lives in a new and positive direction. Their shirts are printed by homeless individuals from surrounding shelters. Ashbury provides them with a means of income that assists them in building their self-esteem and helps get them off the streets and back into society.

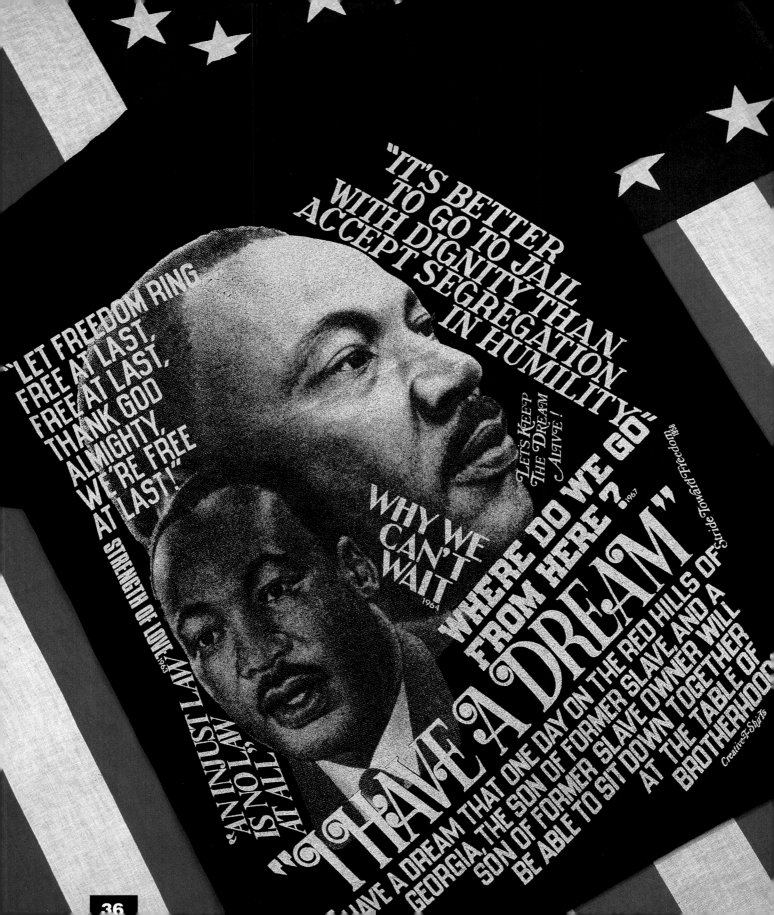

LIVING IN THE '90s
Don't breathe the air
Don't drink the water
Don't eat fruit, vegetables, meat,
fish, sugar, salt, fats
Don't have sex ever again
Have a nice day

▼ **ENDANGERED SPECIES** are but a few of the causes promoted on T-shirts. This marvelous image is from Ron Busbee's 2000 Street Graphics line of Activistwear.

▲ **YES, THIS IS** the nineties, and look how the world has changed from the sixties! Can we still have a nice day with such a grim outlook on life?

◀ **THIS IS A MARVELOUS** print in gold ink on a black shirt. Its message repeats the words of the late Dr. Martin Luther King. "I have a dream" are also the words of Ben Nelson of Creative Tees in Miami, FL . He printed 20,000 of these shirts for a convention and then sold all 20,000—grossing over $100,000 in two weeks.

▼ **THIS WHIMSICAL** "save the planet" shirt gets the message across that there is lots to be done.

Shirt copyright Lunatic Fringe, Little Rock, AR.

▲ **NOW HERE IS A REAL MESSAGE.** This line of shirts, from Just Ask in Pittsburgh, PA, is called LoF Inactive Wear. The message is simple. These shirts are to be worn when you are inactive and just plain loafing. As their promotional material states, these shirts are to be worn when you are not playing tennis, basketball, lifting weights, or otherwise being active. LoF Inactive Wear is the official clothing of Craig T. Nelson's (of TV's *Coach* fame) Screaming Eagles.

THE NINETIES HAVE SEEN AN EXPLOSION of religious T-shirts. Not to be content with just slogans, the printers at Solid Light in Columbus, OH, have come up with terrific graphics to go with slogans and scriptures. Designs © Solid Light.

CHAPTER 7

T-Shirts in the Workplace

The only place where a T-shirt may not be fashionable is at the office in corporate America. This is changing though. The pressure is on to make the corporate workplace more relaxed and egalitarian.

In the past five years, nearly two-thirds of U.S. companies have relaxed their dress codes, allowing casual-dress days, according to a study conducted by the Society of Human Resources Management in Alexandria, Virginia.

Fridays are now officially dress-down days at companies such as Motorola Inc., AlliedSignal Inc., Dial Corp., American Express Co., and IBM.

In fact, in 1994 the government's Central Intelligence Agency made trench coats, ties, and nylons optional on Fridays. It may still be awhile, though, before they let employees wear imprinted shirts with the initials CIA.

Some companies have moved dress-down Fridays to dress-down everyday. Southwest Airlines started in 1986 with its "fun wear." This evolved into casual summers and finally to full-time casual.

The change to casual wear has had a major effect on the suit makers of the world. In 1994 men purchased only 13 million suits, down from 14.6 million in 1989, according to NPD Group Inc., a New York-based research company.

While a T-shirt and jeans may not yet be accepted by some major corporations, it is a way of life for the average workingman. In fact, the printed T-shirt has become an inexpensive uniform. T-shirts with company names, product names, and logos are the mainstay of screen printers nationwide. Even the customers want these shirts. What other advertising medium is there where you don't have to pay someone to promote your product or company?

IN 1975, THE PHOENIX
Fire Department made history when it became the first fire department in the U.S. to adopt as their official uniform the now-traditional navy blue T-shirt with white fire department printing on it. This look, along with a traditional Maltese on the front, is now found on almost every firefighter in the U.S.

Photo courtesy of Phoenix Fire Department. Firefighters Angel Herrera, David Acero, and Sue Rutledge at work.

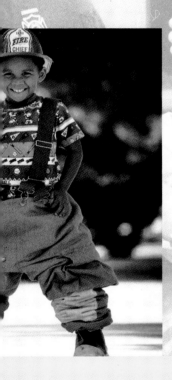

▲ **LOGO SHIRTS** with company or product names are the mode of dress for thousands of companies.

Shirts courtesy of Titus Titanium. Models: Hal and Sue Reneau.

▲ **EVEN A FIREMAN'S SON,**
James Thompson, has to get into the act.

Photo courtesy of Signature Model and Talent Agency, Phoenix, AZ.

◄ Open shirt courtesy of Phoenix Fire Department; folded shirts courtesy of Paradise California Fire Department.

Entertainment, the Arts, and Rock 'n' Roll

Promoters are always looking for ways to make an easy dollar when promoting a movie, TV show, act, or entertainer—and no other method has been more popular than printed T-shirts. Even theatergoers buy T-shirts as mementos of plays or musicals they have attended. The two most cherished event souvenirs are a ticket stub and T-shirt.

Many of us can remember standing in a throng of bodies to get to the T-shirt booth to spend $25 for our official Pink Floyd or Rolling Stones T-shirts. After all, they may never tour again!

While rock 'n' roll has been at the forefront of T-shirt sales, even country-western artists have gotten into the act. Rock fans seem to prefer black T-shirts with outrageous designs. Country fans generally opt for a more conservative "photo on a shirt" look on a white background.

One of the largest suppliers of rock 'n' roll T-shirts is Winterland Productions in San Francisco. Founded by the late Bill Graham in 1972, Winterland was one of the first printers to do terrific graphics on black shirts and initiated the concept of tour merchandise in the early seventies. After starting out by selling Grateful Dead shirts in the lobby at Winterland concerts in San Francisco, the company now boasts over 500 employees and can print 150,000 shirts per day! Winterland is now owned by MCA Music Entertainment Group.

The rock 'n' roll and country-western T-shirt business is dominated by large companies such as Winterland, Brockum, Sony Signatures, and others who are prepared to ship vast quantities of printed T-shirts to all parts of the country on very short notice to meet the demand of souvenir-crazy concertgoers.

During the busy concert season, these printers have tractor trailers lined up at one door unloading thousands of dozens of blank shirts, and tractor trailers being loaded with thousands of dozens of printed shirts out another door—every day! Shirts are printed on large automatic presses costing $100,000 or more that can reproduce up to fourteen colors at a time. Companies such as Winterland have dozens of these automatic presses running twenty-four hours each day.

THE T-SHIRT INDUSTRY owes a large debt of gratitude to producer Steven Spielberg, whose movies such as *Jaws, Raiders of the Lost Ark,* and *Close Encounters* have accounted for millions of great T-shirt designs. During the summer of 1993, dinosaur-crazy people bought millions of *Jurassic Park* shirts. This design is called an "all-over" print because it covers the entire garment. It is also called a "belt print" by the screen-printing industry because the shirt is placed on a large conveyor belt when printed. The shirt is positioned on the belt, using laser lights.

Shirt copyright Changes, New York City, NY. Design trademark Amblin Entertainment.

▼ **FROM BELUSHI** to the Coneheads, *Saturday Night Live* is immortalized on T-shirts.

Shirts courtesy of Scott Fresener collection.

▲ **THE MTV GENERATION** loves them. Parents hate them.

Beavis and Butt-Head all-over print copyright MTV Productions.

SHIP OF FOOLS? Not really, when you count the money made by a group of sixties musicians who are still playing and selling shirts in the nineties.
Shirt copyright Grateful Dead Merchandise.

▼ BROADWAY MUSICALS make a
large portion of profits from merchandise. *The Phantom
of the Opera* shirt is printed with a special ink that makes
the mask glow in the dark.

Shirts courtesy of Asha Gopal collection.

▲ FROM HIPPIE ROCK to the British
invasion to punk rock.

Shirts copyright Grateful Dead Merchandise and Brockum.

▶ A PINK FLOYD FAN wouldn't be
without a souvenir shirt. (This one is from the author's
private collection.) Any group who can be on the *Billboard*
Top 200 chart for 724 weeks and can gross $62 million for
1994/95 tours deserves a hot graphic. A Floyd fan would
not want to miss out on the shirt from the last tour! $25
for a shirt that costs $3 wholesale! That's marketing! T-
shirts and rock 'n' roll are like milk and cereal. You can't
have one without the other. The song of T-shirt printers
everywhere—"Hail, Hail, Rock 'n' Roll."

▼ **WHILE BLACK** is the color of rock 'n' roll, white with a photo-realistic image has become the symbol of the more adult, country-western crowd. These terrific images are part of the award-winning prints from Andy Anderson at Anderson Studios, Nashville, TN.

▲ **EVEN DEAD MUSICIANS** still
▶ sell shirts. Bob Marley and Jim Morrison fans can never get enough of their images.

Bob Marley shirt from Mike Fresener collection.
Jim Morrison airbrush shirt from Top Gun Airbrush, Tucson, AZ.

CHAPTER 9

Sports and T-Shirts

The T-shirt and sports have had a very happy marriage from the beginning. The shirt was the perfect garment to wear while playing sports in the hot summer, and it could easily be screen printed with a team name and number.

In early spring, many young boys and girls proudly display their Little League T-shirt to friends and family—and every spring, screen printers print millions of shirts with numbers and names. The same goes for soccer, hockey, and any other sport in which team affiliation is important.

As youngsters get older, they start to purchase shirts of pro teams displaying logos. Now we are talking about serious money. In fact, the licensing of pro-team logos has turned from a nice little business into a billion-dollar industry with its own licensing trade shows, trade magazines, and associations. In fact, revenues from sports licensing was almost $14 billion in 1994!

Unfortunately, the T-shirt business can be hard hit financially by the whims of the sports market. The baseball strike of 1994–95 caused many of the largest printers to show losses for the first time, and some even went out of business.

Screen printers tend to be very entrepreneurial and will often lose the farm on the drop of a touchdown pass or the miss of a basket. Even new sports franchises take great risks. When Major League Baseball awarded the Arizona Diamondbacks a baseball franchise in the spring of 1995, the baseball strike was not yet over. The team was unable to sell the expected $1 million in T-shirts—they sold only $300,000 worth.

The real impact on sports logo shirts came in the late eighties, when Jon Weiss's New Buffalo Shirt Factory, based in New York, teamed with an artist named Dave Gardner. Their lifelike photo-realistic images on black shirts became the hot properties. (The T-shirt trade magazines called them "the kings of the black shirts.") With the marketing of companies such as Salem Sportswear, the entire industry graduated from simply putting team names on shirts to producing T-shirts with exciting graphics that people couldn't get enough of.

The collegiate market is also a major purchaser of T-shirts. In the sixties and seventies, the universities hadn't noticed that all of the local screen printers were making lots of money printing school mascots onto T-shirts. Once the universities got wise—and trademarked their logos—licensing their rights became big business. Companies such as Collegiate Licensing Corporation now monitor and administer licensing programs for all of the major universities. Printers who want to sell college mascots on shirts have to go through a lengthy licensing process and pay up to 7 ½ percent of the wholesale sales to the school.

Designs copyright Magic Johnson Tees, Salem Sportswear, Front Pages, Starter Sportswear.
Designs and logos trademarked by NBA, NFL, MLB.

DESIGNS and great printing like this really created a demand for sports T-shirts.

Design from Gardner Graphics. Printing by New Buffalo T-shirt Factory for Salem Sportswear. Trademark and copyright NFL.

▼ **FROM 1985 TO 1995 . . .**

the evolution of a Super Bowl souvenir T-shirt.

Trademarks and copyrights National Football League. Shirts by Logo 7, Salem Sportswear, and Starter.

▲ **GIRLS GET INVOLVED** in team sports, too, and the shirts are a central part of the outfit.

Model: Lora Kukral, Dani's Agency, Phoenix, AZ.

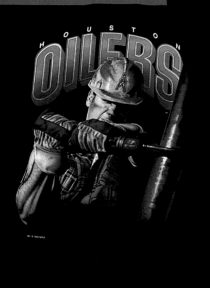

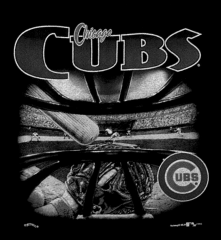

▲ **FROM SIMPLE TWO-COLOR**
graphics in 1983 to photo-realism on black shirts in 1995.

Oilers design copyright New Buffalo T-shirt Factory and Salem
Sportswear; Cubs shirt copyright Nutmeg Mills; Dallas Cowboys from
Scott Fresener collection. Trademarks and copyrights NFL and MLB.

EVEN $300,000 WORTH of a ▶
new baseball franchise shirt isn't bad—especially with a
baseball strike still on in the spring of 1995!

Design copyright Arizona Diamondbacks. Trademark and copyright MLB.
Newspaper copyright *The Arizona Republic.*

▼ **A SOUVENIR** to cherish.

From the David Holderbach collection.

▲ **THE FRONT PAGES** specializes in printing the front page of the local newspaper on T-shirts when the headline will guarantee sales. These shirts were on the streets at 6:00 A.M. on the morning the paper hit, and 10,000 shirts were sold in seven days.

Shirt copyright Front Pages. Trademark NBA. Newspaper copyright *The Arizona Republic.*

Lawrence Taylor

first time... last time... only time...

WF
WRESTLEMANIA
XI

◄ **THE WORLD WRESTLING FEDERATION** has a great focus: They provide family entertainment—and sell lots of T-shirts, too!

Shirts by Pure Art, USA. Trademarks and design copyright World Wrestling Federation.

ASU
un Devils

► **COLLEGIATE LICENSING** is big business, but here's the real question: Is the Arizona State University mascot, Sparky, really the likeness of Walt Disney? In 1946, when Disney artist Bert Anthony designed the mascot (for $75), rumor has it that he used the face of Walt Disney as his guide. You be the judge. Like many universities, ASU did not trademark the logo at the time, and the oversight caused many problems when the licensing craze hit in the seventies and eighties.

Shirt courtesy Arizona Images, Tempe, AZ.

CHAPTER 10

Souvenir, Commemorative, and Collectible T-Shirts

The T-shirt is like a camera. You buy shirts to show where you have been and what you have done. They are a souvenir of a trip you've taken or a race you've run, or a disaster you've survived. The T-shirt is a symbol that you were there. You can tell fellow shoppers at the market that you went to Hawaii without ever saying a word. Some people show off their shirts like a photo album—remembering specifics about the shirt, where and how they got it, and what the design is all about.

The T-shirt is the gift that keeps giving. As long as you buy it large enough, you will make every recipient happy. Then the receivers can act like they went to Hawaii—without ever leaving the mainland!

Unfortunately, T-shirts eventually wear out. Once they have served the gratification of the moment, you buy another one that is newer and better. Old shirts go to the bottom of the drawer, and you bring them out to wear when mowing the lawn. Eventually they become dust rags, and you finally just throw them away. For this reason it is very hard to find older shirts. Sure, there are thousands of new shirts with old designs. It's easy to find shirts with pictures of the early Beatles—but to find one that is an original from that time period is very hard.

Shirt collectors are a rarity. Go to any antique store or show and you can find everything but T-shirts. Old Coke bottles—now there's an antique—but a T-shirt is just a T-shirt. Maybe some day T-shirts will get traded like baseball cards. I'll trade a 1994 Super Bowl for a 1994 World Series. (Now there's a shirt that would be worth money!)

A $26,000 T-SHIRT? This has got to be one of the most expensive shirts ever! In commemoration of the 1996 Olympics, Hanes produced 500 specially numbered and printed limited-edition T-shirts to be auctioned off at the rate of one shirt per day for the 500 days preceding the '96 Olympics. The first shirt was sold on March 7, 1995, for a record $26,000 to Brad Shuman of San Diego, CA. All of the proceeds are going to charity and to help the U.S. Olympic Team.

Design copyright Hanes. Auction photo courtesy of Mahan Photography, Lilburn, GA.

WHEN RUMOR HAD IT THAT THERE WAS A COLLECTOR WITH OVER 1,000 SHIRTS right in my backyard in Phoenix, I said, "impossible!" Was I surprised when I met Waldo (Paul Stewart). We spent the good part of a day going through boxes and drawers full of shirts that were all neatly folded. I felt like I was going through Waldo's life history. The interesting thing about Waldo is that he has been a paraplegic since 1985, when an ATV flipped over on him. This, after years of living on the edge as a sky diver. His handicap doesn't stop him from being a single parent to an eight-year-old daughter and riding his motorcycle (with sidecar for his daughter) to weekly runs, shows, and events. It took us months to find time in his busy schedule to shoot photos of him and his shirts! This photograph represents only a quarter of his entire collection.

THIS IS NOT EXACTLY the collectible you would think, but for some it is worth $25 to have a shirt with the signature of Pete Best. Who is Pete Best? If you are old enough, you'll know that he was the first drummer of the Beatles—before Ringo Starr. The design is from the Cavern Club in London, where the Beatles first played.

REAL COLLECTIBLES are one-of-
a-kind airbrush shirts. They are generally found in mall
T-shirt stores, along beach boardwalks, and at fairs. Jo Ann
Mauck and husband Byron operate Art Attacks Ink, an airbrush T-shirt store in Arizona, and travel around the country working fairs in the summer. Jo Ann's spectacular
images of rock stars and animals sell for $100 and higher.

SIM & HOPP

19**SM**92

ALIDEBERGSBADET
BORÅS

JAMAICA

FLUGLEIÐIR
INNANLANDS

Eat the Beat!

CEBU

cayo largo
cuba

I SURVIVED
HONG KONG

POCO LOCO
CLUB

GUADALAJARA

LES CIGARES
DU PHARAON

Guam U.S.A.

◀ **A GREAT PRINT** that combines special inks that puff, feel like suede, and shine like foil.

Shirt courtesy of Maiden West, Phoenix, AZ.

▶ **WHEN YOU ARE IN THE SERVICE,** you want to brag about your military affiliation. No one wants to mess with a marine.

◀ **PRINTED T-SHIRTS** from around the world. We don't know what most of them say, but they sure look like souvenirs.

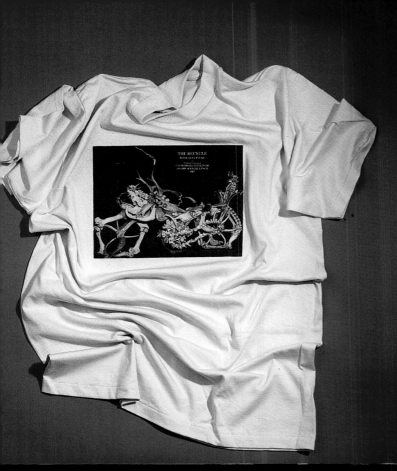

◀ **NOT ONLY DOES BILL HARRINGTON FIGHT FIRES** —and actually print souvenir shirts at the fire line—he is also into motorcycles. His famous bone sculpture, "The Recycle," has won numerous awards and is a popular attraction at the Sturgis, South Dakota, Black Hills Bike Rally.

Shirt and print courtesy of Bill's Enterprises, Valley Springs, CA.

▶ **A TRIP TO WHISKEY ROW** in Prescott, AZ, wouldn't be complete without a Bird Cage Saloon T-shirt. Just check your gun at the door.

Shirt courtesy of Whisky Row Grafix, Prescott, AZ.

◀ **NOW HERE IS A CONCEPT:**
▼ Disaster Wear Shirts from California. (You couldn't have picked a better state.) This collection of T-shirts is by Jamie DeMatoff. You may have seen Jamie and his special line of O. J. Simpson Trial T-shirts featured on *Entertainment Tonight, A Current Affair, Inside Edition, Hard Copy, 20/20* . . . and the list goes on. His earthquake, flood, and fire shirts sell well, too.

Shirts courtesy of Disaster Wear, Sherman Oaks, CA.

◀ **SPEAKING OF**
▶ **STURGIS,** you just don't ride
a Harley without having a few dozen different Harley shirts—one for each ride
or event you have attended.

Harley Untamed Shirt courtesy of R. K. Stratton.
Trademark Harley-Davidson Motorcycle Co.
Sturgis shirts courtesy of—you guessed it—Waldo.

◀ **RATHER THAN JUST ONE**
shirt for a specific place, why not cover the entire state
with a map shirt? Then you could be anywhere, and, if you
get lost, just look at the shirt.

CHAPTER 11

Slogan Shirts

Everyone loves a good laugh and slogan shirts don't require much thinking to understand them. Just a quick read and a smirk or belly laugh. This is a small sampling of the many thousands of great slogan shirts.

MACHINE WASH COLD
TUMBLE DRY LOW
DO NOT BLEACH
FIGHT THE POWER
DO NOT IRON DECORATION
DO NOT PET STRAY DOGS
© LUNATIC FRINGE, INC.
LITTLE ROCK, AR

CHAPTER 12

Terrific, Outstanding, Unique, and Outrageous T-Shirts!

This is what makes the T-shirt business fun! Now that graphic designers have found a great canvas, there is just no end to the terrific shirts being printed. This section has a small handful of some of the thousands of outstanding shirt designs printed each year.

Even after being in the business for over twenty-five years, I love to see a shirt and chuckle—or maybe even laugh out loud—or better yet, to just marvel at the state of the art in printing quality and graphic design!

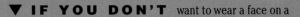

▼ **IF YOU DON'T** want to wear a face on a shirt—how about an animal?

These marvelous prints are from Mirror Image, Cambridge, MA.

The Nighthawks (1942)

Edward Hopper

▼ **EVEN CLASSIC PRINTS** like
◄ *Nighthawks 1942* and underwater scenes like *The Cosmos*
from Christian Lassan look great on T-shirts.

Shirts courtesy Pure Art, USA. The Cosmos copyright Christian Lassan.

◄ **IF YOU LIKE CARS,** you probably
have a Tedder design from Andy's Tees. They are undoubt-
edly the best car designs around! This detailed image,
called "Pepsi Timeless," won the 1993 *ScreenPlay
Magazine* Terrific T-Shirt Contest.

Design by Greg Tedder. Shirt courtesy Andy's Tees, Concord, CA.

THE COSMOS

◀ **LOOKS GOOD ENOUGH TO EAT!**

Shirt courtesy of Pure Art, USA, Scottsdale, AZ.

▶ **SHOW YOUR SUDS** with beer shirts!

I've Fallen And I
Can't Reach
My Beer!

LOBOTOMY
BEER
IN THE MORNING YOU'LL WISH YOU HAD NO BRAIN!

have
another
beer

MOURNING DOVE NORTHERN CARDINAL CHIMNEY SWIFT ROCK DOVE, PIGEON

EUROPEAN STARLING COMMON RAVEN RED-HEADED WOODPECKER BARN SWALLOW

CALIFORNIA GULL RED-WINGED BLACKBIRD COMMON GRACKLE BLUE JAY

AMERICAN ROBIN CAROLINA CHICKADEE RUBY-THROATED HUMMINGBIRD

HOUSE SPARROW YELLOW WARBLER NORTHERN MOCKINGBIRD

EYEWITNESS BOOKS
BIRD
Discover the world of a bird in close-up—
its natural history, behavior,
courtship habits, and secret life

THE PERFECT GIFT FOR BIRD-WATCHERS.

One of the many great concept shirts from the creative minds of MINC.,
Champaign, IL.

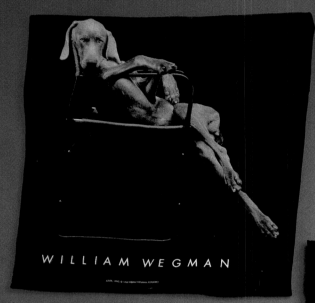

WILLIAM WEGMAN

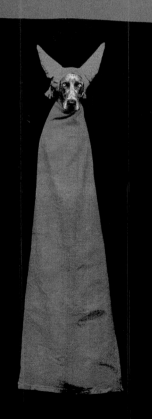

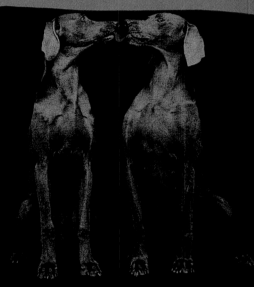

WILLIAM WEGMAN

on T-shirts? You, too, can own a Picasso for only $20.

Shirts courtesy Pure Art, USA, Scottsdale, AZ.

▲ DOG LOVERS EVERYWHERE

◄ delight at the famous William Wegman Weimaraner dogs
in crazy poses. These must be either patient dogs or they
have patient owners.

Award-winning prints by Mirror Image, Cambridge, MA. Designs copyright
William Wegman.

SANDY SKOGLUND
REVENGE OF THE GOLDFISH

SANDY SKOGLUND
RADIOACTIVE CATS

SOMEONE LAID AWAKE at night thinking up these outrageous designs from Sandy Skoglund.

Shirts courtesy of Mirror Image, Cambridge, MA. Copyright Sandy Skoglund.

JUST WALK INTO any Natural Wonder store and find lifelike animal prints like these.

Tiger shirt copyright Nature Store; Endangered Species copyright Habitat; Giraffe shirt copyright Yankee Trader, Singapore.

SOME OF THE MOST BIZARRE art you'll ever find on shirts comes from the Marino Brothers and Carcas Covers in Milwaukee. The mix of rock, action, and cartoon themes with dyed backgrounds make for a truly wild look. Their specialty is a splatter bleach process, and they do all the printing on manual printing equipment.

Designs copyright Carcas Covers.

CARCASS COVERS

(Kär' kes Kuv' ers). noun . words, which when combined, describe a new means of pleasing the mind and body by clothing it in cool visual imagery. 1. To shroud one's body (living or dead) with dramatic, stimulating artwork. 2. A wearable object bearing strange or unpredictable images, to be worn by males and females.

83

The following list contains words and phrases that are commonly used in the T-shirt industry.

AIRBRUSH
A tool used to spray liquids or inks by means of compressed air.

BLACK AND WHITE
Artwork that is prepared on a white background using black pens, markers, etc.

BLEED
Image areas that are printed beyond the edge of the substrate. Often confused with "blend."

BLEEDING
1. The spreading of ink into an area where it is not supposed to be.
2. The spreading of garment dyes into the print.

BLEND
Printing: The use of more than one color in the same screen to create a multicolor effect. Garments: a blend of yarn such as 50 percent cotton and 50 percent polyester.

BURN
To expose an image into a screen-printing screen.

CALENDERING
A preshrinking method using steam to bring fabric to the correct width.

CAROUSEL
A common term applied to a manual, multicolor, T-shirt printing press with screens that can move or spin horizontally.

CLIP ART
Artwork that is camera-ready and copyright-free for use in designs.

CLOGGING
The drying of ink in the screen.

COLOR SEPARATIONS
Film sets that consist of one film positive for each subtractive primary pigment color of magenta, cyan, and yellow, along with black that has been separated from fully colored artwork and converted into tiny halftone dots.

COLOR SEQUENCE
The printing order of each screen in a multicolor job.

COLORFAST
The ability of a print to withstand repeated laundering and cleaning.

COMPACTING
A preshrinkage method that compacts the fabric like crepe paper.

COPYRIGHT
The right to prohibit others from copying works of art, books, or designs.

COURSES
The horizontal lines of thread in knitted material.

CROCKING
The wearing off of a print when rubbed.

CURING
A reaction within an ink—usually chemical—that promotes polymerization.

CYAN	A specific blue color that is one of the three subtractive primary pigment colors.
DARKROOM	A light-tight room that can be used for camera shots or screen coating and drying.
DYE	The colorant used in inks. Dyes are generally soluble in the ink vehicle.
ELECTROSTATIC FLOCKING	The use of an electrostatic charge to drive flock fibers into an adhesive that has been printed on a substrate.
EMBROIDERY	A method of sewing or stitching an image onto a garment.
EMULSION	A photosensitive coating that is used as the stencil material for screens.
EXPOSURE UNIT	A system for burning or exposing an image into a printing screen.
GHOSTING	A double image in a print.
GREIGE GOODS	Knitted fabric that has not been bleached or dyed.
HALFTONING	The conversion of a continuous-tone piece of art or photograph into various-sized dots.
HAND	The way a print feels when touched.
HEAT CURING	The curing of textile inks through heat.
HEAT-TRANSFER	A special screen-printed image on release paper that is applied to a garment with an iron or special heat press.
INK	A general term applied to almost any liquid that can be used to make a print.
INTERLOCK KNIT	A special run-resistant, interlooped knit that has a smooth surface on both sides and makes the garment feel thicker.
IRREGULAR	A garment that is not quite up to mill specifications.
JERSEY KNIT	The standard interlooping of yarn for T-shirt fabric. Also called a "Plain Knit."
KNITTING	Material that is made by interlooping yarn.
LINE ART	A piece of artwork that has no continuous tones and is comprised of light and dark areas only with no grays in between. Also called "Line Copy" or "Line Drawing."

LINEN TESTER	A magnifier used to count the courses and wales of knitted cloth.
LOGO	A special symbol, lettering style, or graphic that is used in advertising and as a trademark to establish immediate recognition by the customer. Also called "Logotype."
MAGENTA	A blue-red color that is one of the three primary pigment colors.
MATERIAL SAFETY DATA SHEET	(MSDS) Data sheets that are supplied by manufacturers detailing the safe use and handling of specific chemicals and their physical and reactive properties.
MESH	Screen fabric used on a screen-printing frame.
MIGRATION	The movement of ink into another ink, coating, or substrate causing unwanted muddying of colors.
MISPRINT	A print that is not up to quality standards. Also called a "Reject."
OPAQUE	Light proof. Screen-printing inks for black shirts must be opaque.
OPEN-END YARN	The standard yarn used in T-shirt knitting.
OVERLAY	A mechanical or film that is used to create additional colors in a design.
PHOSPHORESCENT INK	Ink that will glow in the dark.
PIGMENT	The particles in ink that give it color.
PIGMENT EMULSION INKS	Inks that contain a pigment mixed with an emulsified vehicle. This includes water-in-oil inks, oil-in-water inks, and some water-based inks.
PLASTISOL	A printing ink most commonly used on garments that contains a plasticizer and resin and will not air-dry or air-cure.
PRIMARY COLORS	The primary colors of light are red, green, and blue. The primary pigment colors are yellow, magenta, and cyan.
PROCESS COLORS	The process ink colors for full-color, process printing of yellow, magenta, and cyan.
PROOF	A sample print.
PUFF INK	An ink that expands when heated and gives an embossed or three-dimensional effect.

REFLECTIVE INK   An ink that has tiny glass beads that reflect light back to its source.

RIB KNIT   Also called a one-by-one Rib Knit and makes a garment more elastic.

RING-SPUN YARN   A fluffier yarn that has an additional step in the spinning process.

SCREEN   The common name given to the "silk screen" used to print on T-shirts.

SECONDARY COLORS   Colors created by overprinting primary colors.

SQUEEGEE   The tool used to push the ink through the screen.

TIE-DYE   A garment-dying method using string or rubber bands to tie the material before it is dyed using vats, sprays, or dye injection. Produces a rainbow multicolor, hand-dyed effect.

VEHICLE   The base used in ink to make it printable.

WALES   The vertical rows of loops on knitted material.

WATER-BASED INK   An ink whose vehicle's binder is soluble in water.

WATER-IN-OILS INK   A textile ink that is made of water, pigments, solvents, and a vehicle that is usually oil.

WEAVING   The fabric-making process of interlacing yarn at right angles.

WEFT   The threads that run the width of the screen fabric.

WICKING   The bleeding of inks or ink additives into the surrounding garment fibers.

WICK GARMENTS   The nature of a fiber to draw moisture away from the body.

YARN   The twisted strands of cotton or cotton/polyester blends of fiber that are used to knit shirts.

YARN NUMBER   The number given to yarn that determines its weight. The higher the number, the thinner the yarn. Yarns can have a single strand or double strand. Most T-shirts are made from a 24- to 36-single yarn.

The following section is just a small selection of major T-shirt industry suppliers.

SCREEN-PRINTING EQUIPMENT MFG.

American M & M
6401 W. Chestnut
Morton Grove, IL 60053
708 967 8530
800 876 1600
708 967 8620 Fax

Chaparral Industries, Inc.
3617 E. LaSalle St.
Phoenix, AZ 85040
602 437 4883
800 654 5885 (U.S.)
602 437 2270 (Fax)

Hopkins International
1336 Seventh St.
Berkeley, CA 94710
510 527 5117
800 233 3385 (California)
800 233 8333 (U.S.)
510 527 1605 (Fax)

Lawson Screen Products
5110 Penrose St.
St. Louis, MO 63115
314 382 9300
800 325 8317
314 382 3012 (Fax)

M & R Printing Equipment, Inc.
1 North 372 Main St.
Glen Ellyn, IL 60137
708 858 6101
800 736 6431
708 858 6134 (Fax)

National Screen Printing Equipment, Inc.
1401 N. Broadway
P.O. Box 105
Pittsburg, KS 66762
316 232 1917
800 843 3928
316 232 1941 (Fax)

R. Jennings Manufacturing Co.
8 Glens Falls Technical Park
Glens Falls, NY 12801
518 798 2277
518 798 3172 (Fax)

Vastex International, Inc.
R D 1 Box 409 D2
Humbolt Industrial Park
Hazelton, PA 18201
717 455 2900
717 455 2927 (Fax)

SCREEN-PRINTING SUPPLIES

A.W.T. World Trade, Inc.
4321 N. Knox Ave.
Chicago, IL 60641
312 777 7100
312 777 0909 (Fax)

Bullseye Screen Print
3720 Revere Street, Unit B
Denver, CO 80239
303 373 2855
800 373 2856
303 373 2737 (Fax)

Calcom Graphic Supply
1822 NE Grand
Portland, OR 97212
503 281 9698
800 452 7432
503 287 0056 (Fax)
(Offices in California also)

California Shirt Sales
800 S. Raymond Ave.
Fullerton, CA 92631
714 879 8590
800 289 7478
714 992 4855 (Fax)
(Offices throughout the western states)

Commercial Screen Supply
6 Kiddie Dr.
Avon Industrial Park
Avon, MA 02322
508 583 2300
800 227 1449 (U.S.)
508 583 8234 (Fax)

Dick Blick
P.O. Box 1267
Galesburg, IL 61402-1267
800 447 8192 (Order Line)
309 343 5785 (Fax)
800 723 2787 (Customer Service)
800 933 2542 (Product Information)
(Offices throughout the country)

Jay Products Co.
2868 Colerain Ave.
Cincinnati, OH 45225-2278
513 541 2514
800 543 4436 (U.S.)
513 541 2552 (Fax)

Kelley & Green
1540 Euclid Ave.
Bristol, VA 24201
703 669 5181
800 336 8761 (U.S.)
703 669 7500 (Fax)

Lambert Co., Inc.
71 Innerbelt Rd.
P.O. Box 209
Somerville, MA 02143
617 628 8150
800 292 2900
617 628 4626 (Fax)

Lawson Screen Print Products
5110 Penrose St.
St. Louis, MO 63115
314 382 9300
800 325 8317
314 382 3012 (Fax)
(Branches throughout U.S.)

Litho-Tech
1921 E. 68th Ave.
Denver, CO 80229-7320
303 288 6837
800 537 6994
303 288 3829 (Fax)

McLogan Supply Co., Inc.
2010 S. Main St.
Los Angeles, CA 90007
213 749 2262
800 540 4072 (California)
213 745 6540 (Fax)
(Also in San Diego)

Nazdar
1087 N. Northbranch St.
Chicago, IL 60622-4292
312 943 8338
800 736 7636
312 943 8215 (Fax)
(Branches throughout U.S.)

Pearl Paint
308 Canal St.
New York, NY 10013
212 431 7932
800 221 6845

Jay Products/Suncoast
4825 140th Ave. North
Clearwater, FL 34622
813 539 7878
800 248 3226
813 538 5185 (Fax)

Texas Screen Process Supply Co.
304 N. Walton
Dallas, TX 75226
214 748 3271
800 366 1776 (U.S.)
214 741 6527 (Fax)

Tubelite Co., Inc.
3111 Bellbrook Dr.
P.O. Box 16456
Memphis, TN 38116
901 396 8320
800 238 5280 (U.S.)
901 396 4648 (Fax)
(Offices throughout the country)

T-SHIRT SUPPLIERS
Major mills and regional wholesalers

Alpha Shirt Co.
401 E. Hunting Park Ave.
Philadelphia, PA 19124
215 291 0300
800 523 4585 (U.S.)
800 845 4970 (Fax)

The Americana Company
18150 S. Figueroa
Gardena, CA 90248
310 354 1380
800 473 2802
310 354 1386 (Fax)

Anvil Knitwear
228 E. 45th St., 4th Floor
New York, NY 10017
212 476 0300
800 223 0332 (U.S.)
212 476 0323 (Fax)

Bodek & Rhodes
2951 Grant Ave.
Philadelphia, PA 19114
215 673 6767
800 523 2721
215 673 3719 (Fax)

Broder Brothers
1255 La Quinta Drive
Building #130
Orlando, FL 32809
407 240 5590
800 521 0850
407 240 0978 (Fax)

California Shirt Sales
800 S. Raymond Ave.
Fullerton, CA 92631
714 879 8590
800 289 7478
714 992 4855 (Fax)

Fruit of the Loom
P.O. Box 90015
Bowling Green, KY 42102-9015
502 781 6400
502 781 6588 (Fax)

Full Line Distributors
2650 Button Gwinnett Dr., #E
Doraville, GA 30367
404 662 3900
800 633 0654
800 432-0799 (Fax)
(Offices throughout the country)

Good Buy Sportswear
2400 31st Street South
P.O. Box 10429
St. Petersburg, FL 33712
813 327 3773
800 282 0974 (U.S.)
813 323 4802 (Fax)

Hanes Printables
P.O. Box 15901
Winston-Salem, NC 27103
910 519 4562
800 685 7557
910 519 4398 (Fax)

J-M Business Enterprises
2244 6th Avenue S.
P.O. Box 3955 Terminal Station
Seattle, WA 98124
206 682 8999
800 678 4200 (U.S.)
206 623 0131 (Fax)

Jewel & Company
9601 Apollo Drive
Landover, MD 20785
301 925 6200
800 638 8583
800 220 7000 (Fax)

Kayman
1333 Lowrie Ave.
S. San Francisco, CA 94080
415 589 8900
800 488 4800
415 589 5686 (Fax)
(Offices throughout the country)

McCreary's Tees
4121 E. Raymond Street
Phoenix, AZ 85040
602 470 4200
800 541 1141
602 470 4207 (Fax)

Mid-America Wholesale
6000 Manchester Trafficway Terr.
Kansas City, MO 64130
816 444 9993
800 366 1416 (U.S.)
816 444 8431 (Fax)

Oneita Industries
P.O. Drawer 24, Conifer St.
Andrews, SC 29510
803 264 5225
800 7 ONEITA
803 264 4262 (Fax)

San-Mar
P.O. Box 529
Preston, WA 98050
206 727 3230
800 426 6399
800 828 0554 (Fax)

SPECIALTY TRADE MAGAZINES

Airbrush Action
P.O. Box 2052
Lakewood, NJ 08701-8052
908 364 2111
908 367 5908 (Fax)

Embroidery Business News
P.O. Box 5400
Scottsdale, AZ 85261
602 990 1101
602 990 0819 (Fax)

Embroidery/Monogram Business
13760 Noel Rd. #500
Dallas, TX 75240
800 527 0207
214 239 3060
214 419 7825 (Fax)

Stitches Magazine
5660 Greenwood Plaza Blvd. #350
Englewood, CO 80111
303 793 0448
303 793 0454 (Fax)

Impressions Magazine
13760 Noel Rd., #500
Dallas, TX 75240
214 239 3060
800 527 0207
214 419 7825 (Fax)

Imprinting Business
3000 Hadley Rd.
South Plainfield, NJ 07080
908 769 1160
908 769 1171 (Fax)

The Press Magazine
5660 Greenwood Plaza Blvd. #350
Englewood, CO 80111
303 793 0448
303 793 0454 (Fax)

Printwear Magazine
P.O. Box 1416
Broomfield, CO 80038
303 469 0424
303 469 5730 (Fax)

Screen Play Magazine
407 Gilbert Ave.
Cincinnati, OH 45202
513 421 2050
513 421 5144 (Fax)

Screen Print Magazine
407 Gilbert Avenue
Cincinnati, OH 45202
513 421 2050
513 421 5144 (Fax)

Imprintables Today
P.O. Box 5400
Scottsdale, AZ 85261
602 990 1101
602 990 0819 (Fax)

SCHOOLS & TRAINING

Rochester Institute of Technology
College of Imaging Science
P.O. Box 9887
One Lomb Memorial Dr.
Rochester, NY 14623
716 475 5000

Screen Printing Technical Foundation
10015 Main St.
Fairfax, VA 22031-3489
703 385 1417

U.S. Screen Printing Institute
1200 N. Stadem Dr.
Tempe, AZ 85281
602 929 0640
800 624 6532
602 929 0766 (Fax)

TRADE ORGANIZATIONS

Embroidery Trade Association
745 N. Gilbert Road, #124-362
Gilbert, AZ 85234
602 497 1274
602 545 0690 (Fax)

Screenprinting and Graphic Imaging Association
10015 Main St.
Fairfax, VA 22031-3489
703 385 1335
703 273 0456 (Fax)

TRADE SHOWS

APEX
Apparel Printing and Embroidery Expo
55 E. Jackson, #1100
Chicago, IL 60604-4188
303 220 4286

Embroidery Expo
P.O. Box 5400
Scottsdale, AZ 85261
602 990 1101
602 990 0819 (Fax)

The Imprinted Sportswear Show
P.O. Box 801402
Dallas, TX 75380
214 239 3060
800 527 0207
214 419 7825 (Fax)

Screen Print Show
10015 Main St.
Fairfax, VA 22031-3489
703 385 1335
703 273 0456 (Fax)

Imprinted T-Shirt & Actionwear Show
3000 Hadley Rd.
South Plainfield, NJ 07080
908 769 1160
908 769 1171 (Fax)

SCOTT FRESENER has been in the T-shirt business since 1970 and is considered one of the founders of the Imprinted Sportswear industry. Scott and his wife, Pat, wrote the definitive books on garment decorating called *How to Print T-Shirts for Fun and Profit* (1979) and *The Encyclopedia of Garment Printing* (1985). Scott and Pat founded the U.S. Screen Printing Institute in 1979 and have taught over 10,000 people the art and craft of imprinting T-shirts. Scott also writes for T-shirt industry trade magazines and speaks at trade shows. In his spare time, he and his wife show Labrador retrievers. In fact, on any given day you can find as many as eight dogs at the Fresener's office in Scottsdale, Arizona.

EARL SMITH AND NANCY HALL are a husband-and-wife team whose photographic specialty is shooting head shots and composites for actors and talent agencies along with general commercial photography. In their spare time, they also act in feature movies and TV commercials. Earl usually plays a bad guy in the many westerns shot in Arizona and has been shot or killed in more parts than he can count.

In their spare time, you can find the Smith's hiking through the Superstition Mountains or up on the Navajo reservations taking pictures of the beautiful Arizona scenery and Native Americans. They even produced a line of Southwest greeting cards featuring their marvelous photographic images.